S.O.S

Skills On Studying

HELP IS ON THE WAY FOR:

Reading Skills

Written by Marilyn Berry
Pictures by Bartholomew

CHILDRENS PRESS™

CHICAGO

Childrens Press
School and Library Edition

Producers: Ron Berry and Joy Wilt Berry
Editor: Kate Dickey
Consultant: Kathy McBride
Design and Production: Abigail Johnston
Typesetting: Curt Chelin

ISBN 0-516-03232-1
Copyright © 1984 by Marilyn Berry
Institute of Living Skills, Fallbrook, CA
All rights reserved.
Printed in the United States of America.

Is **reading** getting you down?

Hang on! Help is on the way!

If you have a hard time

- reading,
- understanding what you read, and
- getting the most out of your reading,

. . .you are not alone.

Just in case you're wondering...

...why don't we start at the beginning?

WHAT IS READING?

Reading is a form of communicating. It is getting meaning from the printed word. When we read, we try to understand what the writer is trying to tell us.

Reading is a skill that we use many times every day. It is almost impossible for you to get through a day without reading something.

WHY IS READING SO IMPORTANT?

Here are just a few reasons.

- Reading helps you live a full life. It allows you to do many things on your own.

- Reading can warn you of danger.

- Reading is an important tool for learning. It is an easy way to learn about almost anything. No matter what interests you, a book has probably been written about it.

- Reading is a major key to success in school. Almost every school subject requires some reading.

- Reading is a great entertainment. It doesn't have to cost anything.

- You can do it alone or with a friend.

THREE TYPES OF READING MATERIAL

All reading material can be divided into three types: recreational, practical, and textbook. Each type of reading material

- has a different purpose,
- has a different level of difficulty, and
- requires a different reading rate.

Your reading rate is how fast you read. Good readers change their reading rate for each type of material.

Recreational Reading

Recreational reading is reading for fun and enjoyment. Some examples are
- fiction
- poetry
- humor
- magazines

The main purpose of recreational reading is to give you pleasure. Choose reading materials that are interesting and enjoyable to you.

Rose Hill Elementary School Library
Rose Hill, Virginia

Recreational reading materials usually do not require slow, careful reading. When you are reading for enjoyment, your reading rate will be at its fastest.

To make sure you enjoy your recreational reading, remember these two things:
- Don't choose materials that are too difficult for you. You will become frustrated and reading will not be fun.
- You do not have to finish everything you start to read. If you do not enjoy the material you choose, set it aside. Try to find something more interesting.

Practical Reading

Practical reading is reading that is used in everyday life. Some examples are
- signs
- labels
- advertisements
- directions
- telephone books
- dictionaries
- personal notes and letters

The main purpose of practical reading is to make your life safer and simpler.

Most practical reading material requires careful reading. When you read practical material, your reading rate will be slower.

Here are some important things you should know about practical reading:

- Some practical reading materials, such as signs and recipes, use abbreviations and incomplete sentences. It is important to make sure you understand what these mean.

- Some practical reading materials, such as labels and advertisements, put important information in small print or in hard-to-find places. It is a good idea to examine this material carefully.

- You may have to read some practical reading materials more than once. For instance, when reading directions, it is a good idea to do these two things.
  1. Read the directions through one time without stopping.
  2. Start at the beginning and read them through again, one step at a time. The second time through, follow each direction as you read it.

Textbook Reading

Textbook reading is the reading of books that are used to teach you about a specific subject. This type of reading is required most often in school and for schoolwork. Some examples are
- history books
- math books
- science books

The main purpose of textbook reading is to help you learn about a specific subject. By learning to read and understand textbook material, your schoolwork will become easier, and school will become more enjoyable.

Most textbook material introduces new ideas, new information, and new words. It requires careful reading. Special attention must be given to facts and details. When you read textbook material, your reading rate will be slower.

To get the most out of a reading assignment in a textbook, follow these five simple steps:

Step 1. Look Over the Assignment. It will help if you get a basic idea of what the material is about **before** you start to read. Try doing these things:
- Read the title.
- Read the introduction (or the first paragraph).
- Look at the illustrations and their captions.
- Read the headings (any phrases in bold type).
- Read the conclusion (or the last paragraph).

Step 2. Read the Questions. Most textbooks have a list of questions at the end of each chapter. These questions make a great study guide. They tell you what you are expected to learn from your reading. Look over the questions before you read the assignment. Then you will know what information to look for as you read. If there are no questions, try making up some of your own. Questions will come to your mind as you look over the assignment.

Step 3. Read the Assignment. By this time, you should have a general idea of what the assignment is about. You should know what you are expected to learn from it. It is now time to read the assignment. As you read, try to keep in mind the questions you went over in Step 2. When you come to a sentence or paragraph that answers one of these questions, put a check in the margin to mark the place. (If you are not allowed to write in your books, use a paper clip as a marker.)

Step 4. Answer the Questions. When you have carefully read the assignment, answer the questions at the end of the chapter. Try to do this without looking up the answers in the reading assignment.

Step 5. Check Your Answers. After you have answered the questions, check your answers. Remember to look for the marks you made as you were reading. Be sure to correct any mistakes.

Following these five steps will help you to get the most out of your textbook reading assignments.

UNDERSTANDING WHAT YOU READ

Understanding what you read is called comprehension. Since the main purpose of reading is to understand what the writer is trying to say, comprehension skills are very important.

There are two types of comprehension:
1. "Finding the Facts," and
2. "Reading Between the Lines."
Each requires a different skill.

1. Finding the Facts
Your teacher may call this **literal comprehension.**
This skill helps you find and understand facts
that are plainly stated.

31

"Finding the Facts" can be divided into three parts: finding the main idea, finding the "Big Five," and finding the supporting details.

Finding the Main Idea. The main idea is the point that the writer wants you to understand most. Sometimes it is stated plainly in the title, the opening paragraph, or the conclusion. Sometimes you have to look harder. A good way to find the main idea is to ask yourself, "What is the most important point that the writer is trying to make?"

Finding the "Big Five". There are five important questions that will help you to understand what you are reading:

1. *What* happened?
2. *When* did it happen?
3. *Where* did it happen?
4. *Who* did it, or to whom did it happen?
5. *How* did it happen?

HMMM

HE SAYS IT HELPS HIM FIND THE BIG 5 QUESTIONS.

NOW I THINK THEY'RE GOING TOO FAR!

If you can answer these five questions after you have read something, you are understanding most of what you read.

Finding the Supporting Details. Sometimes finding the main idea and answering the ''Big Five'' questions will not include everything in your reading. Any other facts that are important for understanding are called supporting details.

2. Reading Between the Lines

Your teacher may call this **inferential comprehension**. This skill helps you understand something that the writer suggested but did not state plainly. Reading between the lines helps you form your own ideas on the subject.

SKIMMING AND SCANNING

Skimming is a valuable skill that can enhance your reading. Skimming is going over a reading selection quickly and **not** thoroughly. You may actually read only a small part of the selection such as the title, subtitles, and the conclusion. The purpose is to pick out the highlights and to get a general idea of what the selection is about.

Scanning is also a valuable skill that can help your reading. Like skimming, it involves going over reading material quickly and **not** thoroughly. However, scanning is different from skimming. Scanning is used when you are looking for a specific piece of information.

Although skimming and scanning can help your reading, they are not the same thing as reading. When you read, you try to see and understand everything on all pages. When you skim or scan, you are looking at just a few bits of information. Therefore, you cannot understand as much when you skim or scan as when you actually read.

YOU CAN INCREASE
YOUR READING RATE

If you find that you are always behind on your reading assignments, you might be reading too slowly. These things may help you learn to read faster:

- **Practice.** As with most skills, practice can improve your reading rate. The more you read, the better a reader you will become.

- **Read silently.** It takes time to say each word you read. When you read aloud, you cut down on your reading rate.
- **Don't point to or mouth each word.** Neither your finger nor your mouth can move as fast as your eyes.

- **Practice reading phrases.** Your eye can see more than one word at a glance. You do not have to look at each individual word.
- **Try not to reread** unless it is for review. If you do not understand what you are reading, try to concentrate more instead of rereading.

READING TIPS

Here are some reading tips that will help you, no matter what type of reading you do.

Create a good environment for your reading.

- Find a quiet place.
- Use proper lighting.
- Try not to read when you are tired.
- Get comfortable, but stay alert.

Listen to your eyes.

If you have a difficult time reading, your eyes may be trying to tell you something. Eye problems can cause reading problems. Look out for these things:

- Do your eyes often become tired when you read?
- Does the print look blurry?
- Do your eyes itch when you read?
- Do you rub your eyes when you read?

If any of these problems occur as you read, it would be a good idea to have your eyes checked.

Keep a dictionary handy.

When you come across an important word that you do not know and cannot figure out, look it up in a dictionary. Especially when reading textbooks, you will often come across new words. Many books have their own dictionaries in the back of the book called glossaries. Whether you use a dictionary or a glossary, your reading will have more meaning when you understand all of the words.

Learn to be a critic.

You should not believe everything you read. Just because something is in print does not make it true. Learn to ask questions as you read, such as:

- Does this make sense to me?
- Do these facts support other material I have read on this subject?
- When was this written? Are there new facts that should be considered?
- Is the writer a reliable person? Does the writer give both sides of the story?

WARNING!

If you do the things in this book...

ALL RIGHT!

...you can become a better reader!

THE END

About the Author

Marilyn Berry has a master's degree in education with a specialization in reading. She is on the staff as a producer and creator of supplementary materials at the Institute of Living Skills. Marilyn is a published author of books and composer of music for children. She is the mother of two sons, John and Brent.